SHOOTING
Log Book

This Log Book Belongs To

NAME	
PHONE	
EMAIL	
ADDRESS	
NOTES	

SHOOTING *Log Book*

SHOOTING

DATE	Ⓜ Ⓣ Ⓦ Ⓣ Ⓕ Ⓢ Ⓢ TIME
LOCATION	
FIREARM	
RIFLE/SCOPE	
AMMUNITION	
SEATING DEPTH	
DISTANCE	
POWDER	GRAINS
PRIMER	
BRASS	

CONDITIONS

LIGHT	WIND
○ BRIGHT	○ LIGHT
○ HAZY	○ MEDIUM
○ OVERCAST	○ HEAVY
○ CHANGING	○ OTHER

12
9   3
6

12
9   3
6

NOTES

OVERALL RESULTS	○ POOR ○ FAIR ○ GOOD ○ EXCELLENT	☆ ☆ ☆ ☆ ☆

◉ TARGET SIZE _____

TARGET _____

TARGET _____

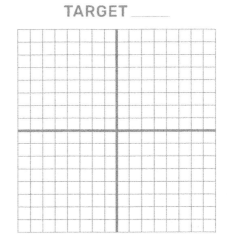

TARGET _____

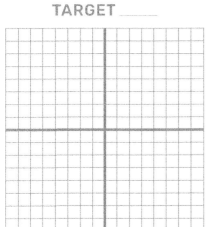

TARGET _____

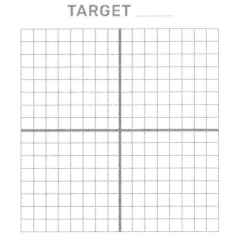

TARGET _____

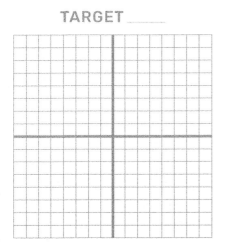

TARGET _____

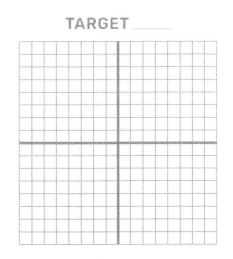

SHOOTING *Log Book*

SHOOTING

DATE	Ⓜ Ⓣ Ⓦ Ⓣ Ⓕ Ⓢ Ⓢ TIME
LOCATION	
FIREARM	
RIFLE/SCOPE	
AMMUNITION	
SEATING DEPTH	
DISTANCE	
POWDER	GRAINS
PRIMER	
BRASS	

CONDITIONS

LIGHT	WIND
○ BRIGHT	○ LIGHT
○ HAZY	○ MEDIUM
○ OVERCAST	○ HEAVY
○ CHANGING	○ OTHER

12
9   3
6

12
9   3
6

NOTES

OVERALL RESULTS	○ POOR ○ FAIR ○ GOOD ○ EXCELLENT	☆ ☆ ☆ ☆ ☆

◎ TARGET SIZE _____

TARGET _____

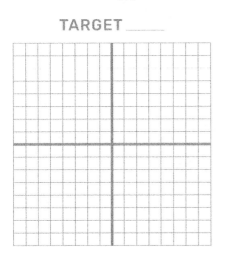

TARGET _____

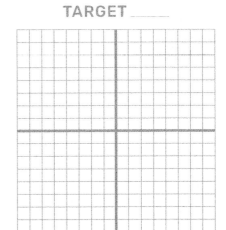

TARGET _____

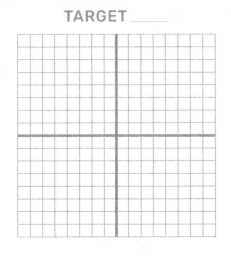

TARGET _____

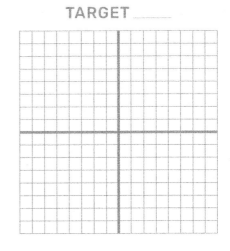

TARGET _____

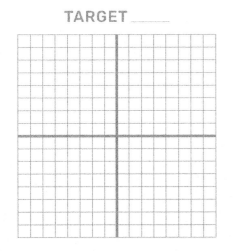

TARGET _____

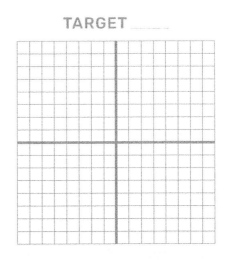

SHOOTING *Log Book*

SHOOTING

DATE	Ⓜ Ⓣ Ⓦ Ⓣ Ⓕ Ⓢ Ⓢ	TIME
LOCATION		
FIREARM		
RIFLE/SCOPE		
AMMUNITION		
SEATING DEPTH		
DISTANCE		
POWDER	GRAINS	
PRIMER		
BRASS		

CONDITIONS

LIGHT	WIND
○ BRIGHT	○ LIGHT
○ HAZY	○ MEDIUM
○ OVERCAST	○ HEAVY
○ CHANGING	○ OTHER

(Light clock: 12, 3, 6, 9)

(Wind clock: 12, 3, 6, 9)

NOTES

OVERALL RESULTS | ○ POOR ○ FAIR ○ GOOD ○ EXCELLENT | ☆ ☆ ☆ ☆ ☆

◎ TARGET SIZE _____

TARGET _____

TARGET _____

TARGET _____

TARGET _____

TARGET _____

TARGET _____

SHOOTING *Log Book*

SHOOTING

DATE		Ⓜ Ⓣ Ⓦ Ⓣ Ⓕ Ⓢ Ⓢ	TIME	
LOCATION				
FIREARM				
RIFLE/SCOPE				
AMMUNITION				
SEATING DEPTH				
DISTANCE				
POWDER		GRAINS		
PRIMER				
BRASS				

CONDITIONS

LIGHT	WIND
○ BRIGHT	○ LIGHT
○ HAZY	○ MEDIUM
○ OVERCAST	○ HEAVY
○ CHANGING	○ OTHER

(LIGHT clock: 12, 3, 6, 9) (WIND clock: 12, 3, 6, 9)

NOTES

OVERALL RESULTS	○ POOR ○ FAIR ○ GOOD ○ EXCELLENT	☆ ☆ ☆ ☆ ☆

TARGET _____

TARGET _____

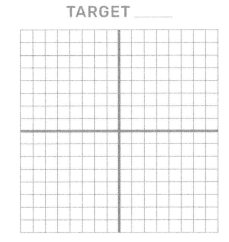

TARGET _____

TARGET _____

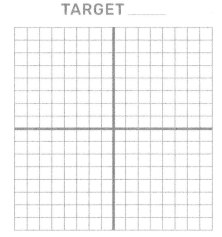
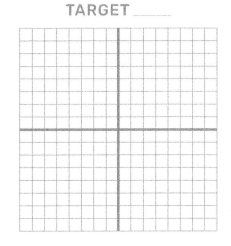

TARGET _____

TARGET _____

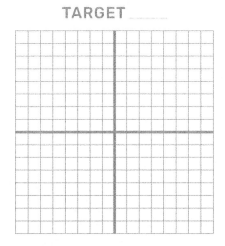
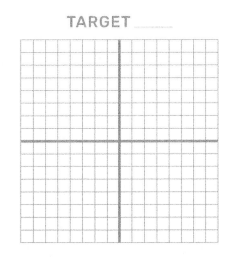

SHOOTING *Log Book*

SHOOTING

DATE	Ⓜ Ⓣ Ⓦ Ⓣ Ⓕ Ⓢ Ⓢ TIME
LOCATION	
FIREARM	
RIFLE/SCOPE	
AMMUNITION	
SEATING DEPTH	
DISTANCE	
POWDER	GRAINS
PRIMER	
BRASS	

CONDITIONS

LIGHT	WIND
○ BRIGHT	○ LIGHT
○ HAZY	○ MEDIUM
○ OVERCAST	○ HEAVY
○ CHANGING	○ OTHER

12
9   3
6

12
9   3
6

NOTES

OVERALL RESULTS ○ POOR ○ FAIR ○ GOOD ○ EXCELLENT ☆ ☆ ☆ ☆ ☆

◎ TARGET SIZE _____

TARGET _____

TARGET _____

TARGET _____

TARGET _____

TARGET _____

TARGET _____

SHOOTING *Log Book*

SHOOTING

DATE	Ⓜ Ⓣ Ⓦ Ⓣ Ⓕ Ⓢ Ⓢ TIME
LOCATION	
FIREARM	
RIFLE/SCOPE	
AMMUNITION	
SEATING DEPTH	
DISTANCE	
POWDER	GRAINS
PRIMER	
BRASS	

CONDITIONS

LIGHT	WIND
○ BRIGHT	○ LIGHT
○ HAZY	○ MEDIUM
○ OVERCAST	○ HEAVY
○ CHANGING	○ OTHER

12
9   3
6

12
9   3
6

NOTES

OVERALL RESULTS	○ POOR ○ FAIR ○ GOOD ○ EXCELLENT	☆ ☆ ☆ ☆ ☆

◎ TARGET SIZE _____

TARGET _____

TARGET _____

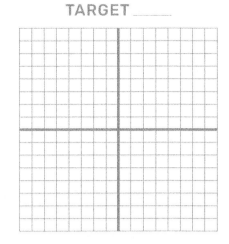

TARGET _____

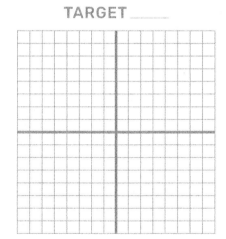

TARGET _____

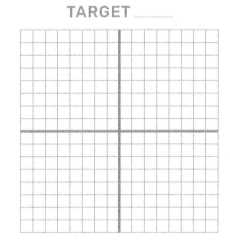

TARGET _____

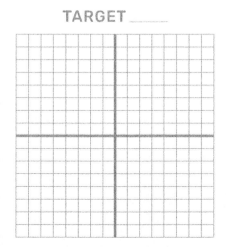

TARGET _____

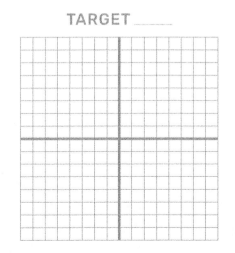

SHOOTING $\mathcal{Log}$ $\mathcal{Book}$

SHOOTING

DATE	Ⓜ Ⓣ Ⓦ Ⓣ Ⓕ Ⓢ Ⓢ TIME
LOCATION	
FIREARM	
RIFLE/SCOPE	
AMMUNITION	
SEATING DEPTH	
DISTANCE	
POWDER	GRAINS
PRIMER	
BRASS	

CONDITIONS

LIGHT	WIND
○ BRIGHT	○ LIGHT
○ HAZY	○ MEDIUM
○ OVERCAST	○ HEAVY
○ CHANGING	○ OTHER

LIGHT — 12, 9, 3, 6

WIND — 12, 9, 3, 6

NOTES

OVERALL RESULTS	○ POOR ○ FAIR ○ GOOD ○ EXCELLENT ☆ ☆ ☆ ☆ ☆

TARGET _____

TARGET _____

TARGET _____

TARGET _____

TARGET _____

TARGET _____

SHOOTING *Log Book*

SHOOTING

DATE	Ⓜ Ⓣ Ⓦ Ⓣ Ⓕ Ⓢ Ⓢ TIME
LOCATION	
FIREARM	
RIFLE/SCOPE	
AMMUNITION	
SEATING DEPTH	
DISTANCE	
POWDER	GRAINS
PRIMER	
BRASS	

CONDITIONS

LIGHT	WIND
○ BRIGHT	○ LIGHT
○ HAZY	○ MEDIUM
○ OVERCAST	○ HEAVY
○ CHANGING	○ OTHER

12 · 9 · 3 · 6

12 · 9 · 3 · 6

NOTES

OVERALL RESULTS | ○ POOR ○ FAIR ○ GOOD ○ EXCELLENT ☆ ☆ ☆ ☆ ☆

◎ TARGET SIZE _____

TARGET _____

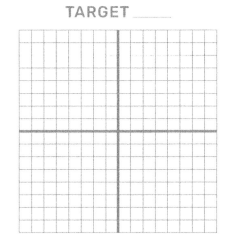

TARGET _____

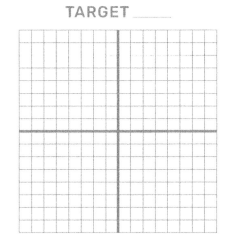

TARGET _____

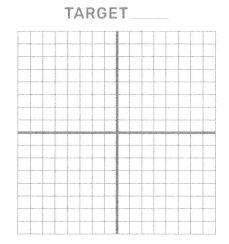

TARGET _____

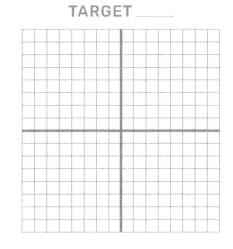

TARGET _____

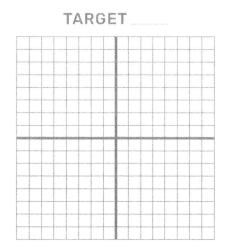

TARGET _____

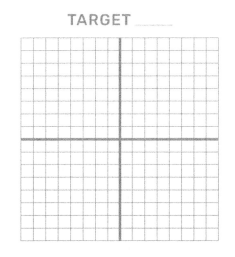

SHOOTING *Log Book*

SHOOTING

DATE	Ⓜ Ⓣ Ⓦ Ⓣ Ⓕ Ⓢ Ⓢ TIME
LOCATION	
FIREARM	
RIFLE/SCOPE	
AMMUNITION	
SEATING DEPTH	
DISTANCE	
POWDER	GRAINS
PRIMER	
BRASS	

CONDITIONS

LIGHT	WIND
○ BRIGHT	○ LIGHT
○ HAZY	○ MEDIUM
○ OVERCAST	○ HEAVY
○ CHANGING	○ OTHER

12
9   3
6

12
9   3
6

NOTES

OVERALL RESULTS ○ POOR ○ FAIR ○ GOOD ○ EXCELLENT ☆ ☆ ☆ ☆ ☆

TARGET _____

TARGET _____

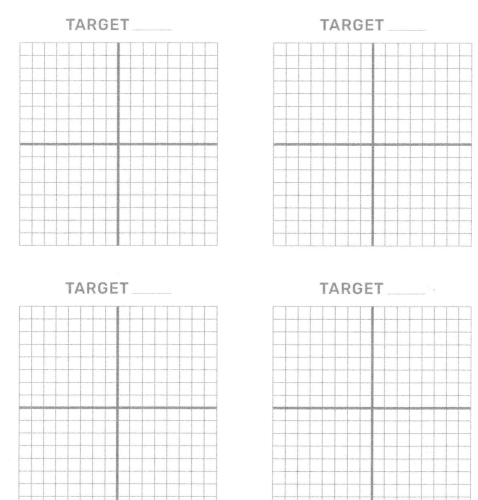

TARGET _____

TARGET _____ .

TARGET _____

TARGET _____

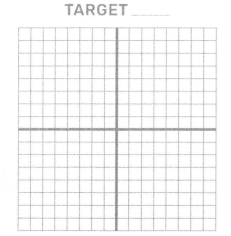
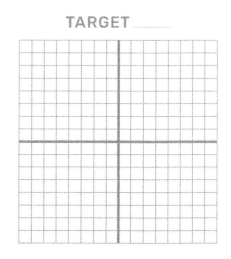

SHOOTING *Log Book*

SHOOTING

DATE	(M)(T)(W)(T)(F)(S)(S) **TIME**
LOCATION	
FIREARM	
RIFLE/SCOPE	
AMMUNITION	
SEATING DEPTH	
DISTANCE	
POWDER	**GRAINS**
PRIMER	
BRASS	

CONDITIONS

LIGHT	WIND
○ BRIGHT 12	○ LIGHT 12
○ HAZY 9 3	○ MEDIUM 9 3
○ OVERCAST	○ HEAVY
○ CHANGING 6	○ OTHER 6

NOTES

OVERALL RESULTS	○ POOR ○ FAIR ○ GOOD ○ EXCELLENT	☆ ☆ ☆ ☆ ☆

TARGET _____

TARGET _____

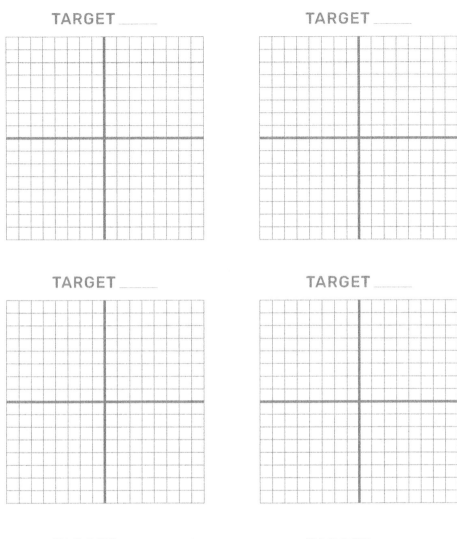

TARGET _____

TARGET _____

TARGET _____

TARGET _____

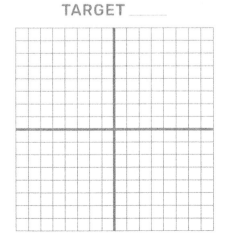
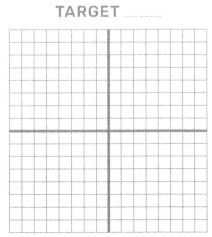

SHOOTING *Log Book*

SHOOTING

DATE	Ⓜ Ⓣ Ⓦ Ⓣ Ⓕ Ⓢ Ⓢ TIME
LOCATION	
FIREARM	
RIFLE/SCOPE	
AMMUNITION	
SEATING DEPTH	
DISTANCE	
POWDER	GRAINS
PRIMER	
BRASS	

CONDITIONS

LIGHT	WIND
○ BRIGHT	○ LIGHT
○ HAZY	○ MEDIUM
○ OVERCAST	○ HEAVY
○ CHANGING	○ OTHER

(clock faces: 12 / 9 / 3 / 6)

NOTES

OVERALL RESULTS	○ POOR ○ FAIR ○ GOOD ○ EXCELLENT ☆ ☆ ☆ ☆ ☆

◎ TARGET SIZE _____

TARGET _____

TARGET _____

TARGET _____

TARGET _____

TARGET _____

TARGET _____

SHOOTING *Log Book*

SHOOTING

DATE	Ⓜ Ⓣ Ⓦ Ⓣ Ⓕ Ⓢ Ⓢ	TIME	
LOCATION			
FIREARM			
RIFLE/SCOPE			
AMMUNITION			
SEATING DEPTH			
DISTANCE			
POWDER		GRAINS	
PRIMER			
BRASS			

CONDITIONS

LIGHT	WIND
○ BRIGHT	○ LIGHT
○ HAZY	○ MEDIUM
○ OVERCAST	○ HEAVY
○ CHANGING	○ OTHER

LIGHT clock: 12, 9, 3, 6
WIND clock: 12, 9, 3, 6

NOTES

OVERALL RESULTS | ○ POOR ○ FAIR ○ GOOD ○ EXCELLENT | ☆ ☆ ☆ ☆ ☆

◎ TARGET SIZE _____

TARGET _____

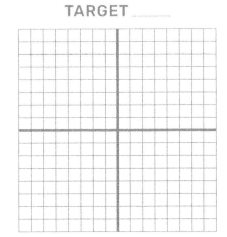

TARGET _____

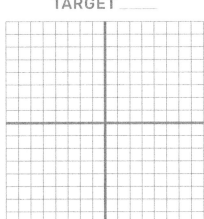

TARGET _____

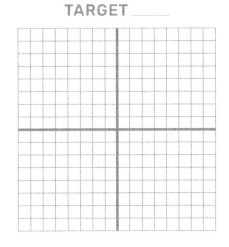

TARGET _____

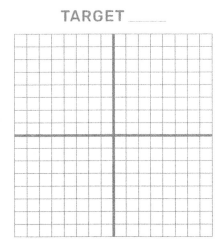

TARGET _____

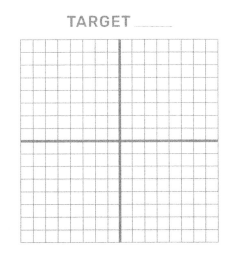

SHOOTING *Log Book*

SHOOTING

DATE	Ⓜ Ⓣ Ⓦ Ⓣ Ⓕ Ⓢ Ⓢ TIME
LOCATION	
FIREARM	
RIFLE/SCOPE	
AMMUNITION	
SEATING DEPTH	
DISTANCE	
POWDER	GRAINS
PRIMER	
BRASS	

CONDITIONS

LIGHT	WIND
○ BRIGHT	○ LIGHT
○ HAZY	○ MEDIUM
○ OVERCAST	○ HEAVY
○ CHANGING	○ OTHER

12
9   3
6

12
9   3
6

NOTES

OVERALL RESULTS	○ POOR ○ FAIR ○ GOOD ○ EXCELLENT	☆ ☆ ☆ ☆ ☆

◉ TARGET SIZE _____

TARGET _____

TARGET _____

TARGET _____

TARGET _____

TARGET _____

TARGET _____

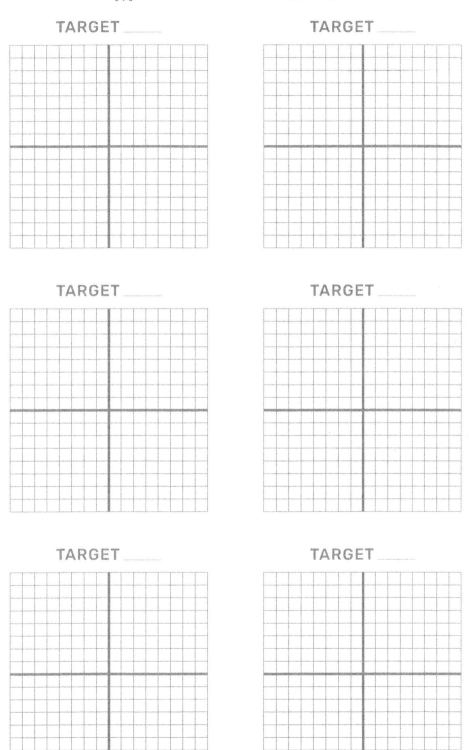

SHOOTING $\mathcal{Log}$ $\mathcal{Book}$

SHOOTING

DATE	Ⓜ Ⓣ Ⓦ Ⓣ Ⓕ Ⓢ Ⓢ TIME
LOCATION	
FIREARM	
RIFLE/SCOPE	
AMMUNITION	
SEATING DEPTH	
DISTANCE	
POWDER	GRAINS
PRIMER	
BRASS	

CONDITIONS

LIGHT	WIND
○ BRIGHT	○ LIGHT
○ HAZY	○ MEDIUM
○ OVERCAST	○ HEAVY
○ CHANGING	○ OTHER

NOTES

OVERALL RESULTS	○ POOR ○ FAIR ○ GOOD ○ EXCELLENT ☆ ☆ ☆ ☆ ☆

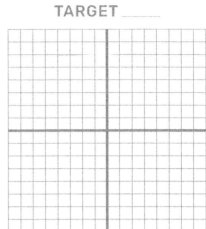

◎ TARGET SIZE _____

TARGET _____

TARGET _____

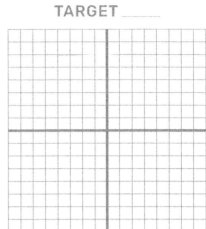

TARGET _____

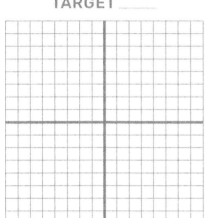

TARGET _____

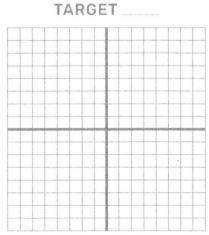

TARGET _____

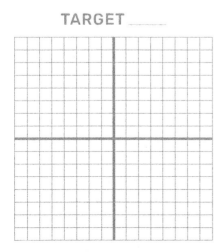

TARGET _____

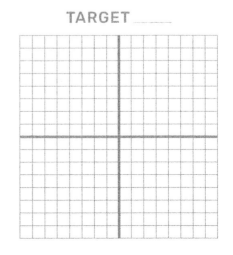

SHOOTING *Log Book*

SHOOTING

DATE	Ⓜ Ⓣ Ⓦ Ⓣ Ⓕ Ⓢ Ⓢ TIME
LOCATION	
FIREARM	
RIFLE/SCOPE	
AMMUNITION	
SEATING DEPTH	
DISTANCE	
POWDER	GRAINS
PRIMER	
BRASS	

CONDITIONS

LIGHT	WIND
○ BRIGHT	○ LIGHT
○ HAZY	○ MEDIUM
○ OVERCAST	○ HEAVY
○ CHANGING	○ OTHER

12
9   3
6

12
9   3
6

NOTES

OVERALL RESULTS | ○ POOR ○ FAIR ○ GOOD ○ EXCELLENT ☆ ☆ ☆ ☆ ☆

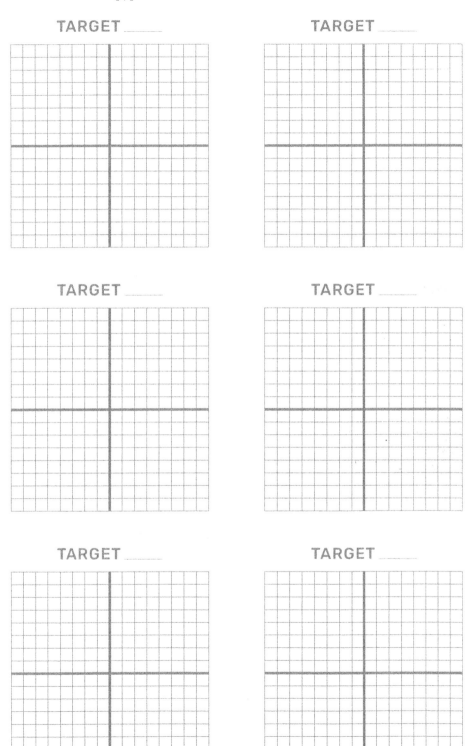

◉ TARGET SIZE _____

TARGET _____

TARGET _____

TARGET _____

TARGET _____

TARGET _____

TARGET _____

SHOOTING ℒog Book

SHOOTING

DATE	Ⓜ Ⓣ Ⓦ Ⓣ Ⓕ Ⓢ Ⓢ TIME
LOCATION	
FIREARM	
RIFLE/SCOPE	
AMMUNITION	
SEATING DEPTH	
DISTANCE	
POWDER	GRAINS
PRIMER	
BRASS	

CONDITIONS

LIGHT	WIND
○ BRIGHT	○ LIGHT
○ HAZY	○ MEDIUM
○ OVERCAST	○ HEAVY
○ CHANGING	○ OTHER

(LIGHT clock: 12, 3, 6, 9)
(WIND clock: 12, 3, 6, 9)

NOTES

OVERALL RESULTS	○ POOR ○ FAIR ○ GOOD ○ EXCELLENT	☆ ☆ ☆ ☆ ☆

TARGET _____

TARGET _____

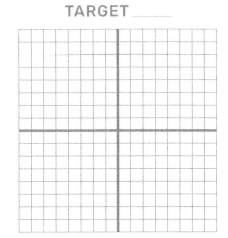

TARGET _____

TARGET _____

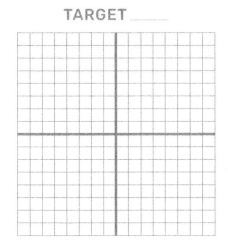

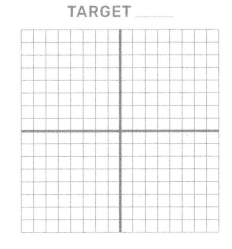

TARGET _____

TARGET _____

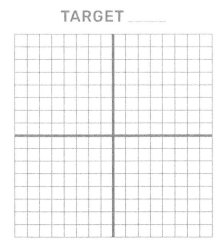

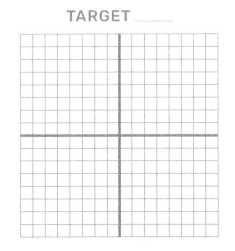

SHOOTING *Log Book*

SHOOTING

DATE	Ⓜ Ⓣ Ⓦ Ⓣ Ⓕ Ⓢ Ⓢ TIME
LOCATION	
FIREARM	
RIFLE/SCOPE	
AMMUNITION	
SEATING DEPTH	
DISTANCE	
POWDER	GRAINS
PRIMER	
BRASS	

CONDITIONS

LIGHT	WIND
○ BRIGHT	○ LIGHT
○ HAZY	○ MEDIUM
○ OVERCAST	○ HEAVY
○ CHANGING	○ OTHER

(clock face: 12, 3, 6, 9) (clock face: 12, 3, 6, 9)

NOTES

OVERALL RESULTS | ○ POOR ○ FAIR ○ GOOD ○ EXCELLENT ☆ ☆ ☆ ☆ ☆

TARGET _____

TARGET _____

TARGET _____

TARGET _____

TARGET _____

TARGET _____

SHOOTING *Log Book*

SHOOTING

DATE	Ⓜ Ⓣ Ⓦ Ⓣ Ⓕ Ⓢ Ⓢ	TIME	
LOCATION			
FIREARM			
RIFLE/SCOPE			
AMMUNITION			
SEATING DEPTH			
DISTANCE			
POWDER		GRAINS	
PRIMER			
BRASS			

CONDITIONS

LIGHT		WIND	
○ BRIGHT		○ LIGHT	
○ HAZY	12	○ MEDIUM	12
○ OVERCAST	9　3	○ HEAVY	9　3
○ CHANGING	6	○ OTHER	6

NOTES

OVERALL RESULTS	○ POOR ○ FAIR ○ GOOD ○ EXCELLENT	☆ ☆ ☆ ☆ ☆

◎ TARGET SIZE _____

TARGET _____

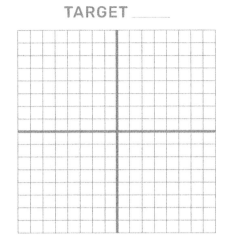

TARGET _____

TARGET _____

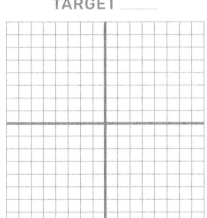

TARGET _____

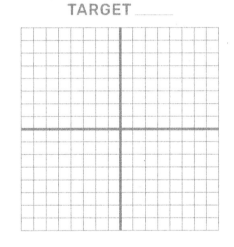

TARGET _____

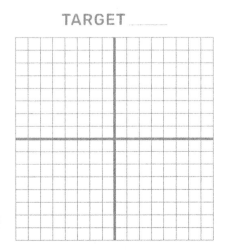

TARGET _____

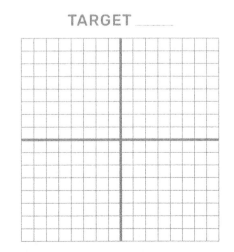

SHOOTING *Log Book*

SHOOTING

DATE	Ⓜ Ⓣ Ⓦ Ⓣ Ⓕ Ⓢ Ⓢ TIME
LOCATION	
FIREARM	
RIFLE/SCOPE	
AMMUNITION	
SEATING DEPTH	
DISTANCE	
POWDER	GRAINS
PRIMER	
BRASS	

CONDITIONS

LIGHT	WIND
○ BRIGHT ○ HAZY ○ OVERCAST ○ CHANGING (12, 3, 6, 9)	○ LIGHT ○ MEDIUM ○ HEAVY ○ OTHER (12, 3, 6, 9)

NOTES

OVERALL RESULTS	○ POOR ○ FAIR ○ GOOD ○ EXCELLENT ☆ ☆ ☆ ☆ ☆

TARGET _____

TARGET _____

TARGET _____

TARGET _____

TARGET _____

TARGET _____

SHOOTING Log Book

SHOOTING

DATE	Ⓜ Ⓣ Ⓦ Ⓣ Ⓕ Ⓢ Ⓢ TIME
LOCATION	
FIREARM	
RIFLE/SCOPE	
AMMUNITION	
SEATING DEPTH	
DISTANCE	
POWDER	GRAINS
PRIMER	
BRASS	

CONDITIONS

LIGHT	WIND
○ BRIGHT	○ LIGHT
○ HAZY	○ MEDIUM
○ OVERCAST	○ HEAVY
○ CHANGING	○ OTHER

LIGHT clock: 12 / 9 / 3 / 6

WIND clock: 12 / 9 / 3 / 6

NOTES

OVERALL RESULTS	○ POOR ○ FAIR ○ GOOD ○ EXCELLENT	☆ ☆ ☆ ☆ ☆

◎ TARGET SIZE _____

TARGET _____

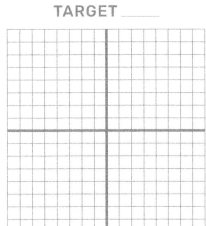

TARGET _____

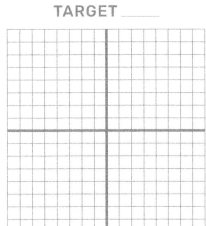

TARGET _____

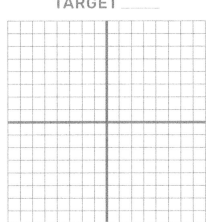

TARGET _____

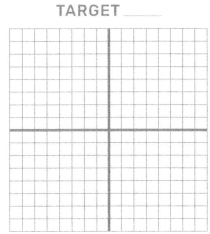

TARGET _____

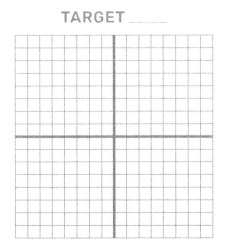

TARGET _____

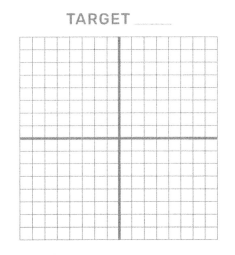

SHOOTING *Log Book*

SHOOTING

DATE	Ⓜ Ⓣ Ⓦ Ⓣ Ⓕ Ⓢ Ⓢ TIME
LOCATION	
FIREARM	
RIFLE/SCOPE	
AMMUNITION	
SEATING DEPTH	
DISTANCE	
POWDER	GRAINS
PRIMER	
BRASS	

CONDITIONS

LIGHT	WIND
○ BRIGHT	○ LIGHT
○ HAZY	○ MEDIUM
○ OVERCAST	○ HEAVY
○ CHANGING	○ OTHER

LIGHT clock: 12, 9, 3, 6

WIND clock: 12, 9, 3, 6

NOTES

OVERALL RESULTS	○ POOR ○ FAIR ○ GOOD ○ EXCELLENT ☆ ☆ ☆ ☆ ☆

TARGET _____

TARGET _____

TARGET _____

TARGET _____

TARGET _____

TARGET _____

SHOOTING Log Book

SHOOTING

DATE	Ⓜ Ⓣ Ⓦ Ⓣ Ⓕ Ⓢ Ⓢ TIME
LOCATION	
FIREARM	
RIFLE/SCOPE	
AMMUNITION	
SEATING DEPTH	
DISTANCE	
POWDER	GRAINS
PRIMER	
BRASS	

CONDITIONS

LIGHT	WIND
○ BRIGHT	○ LIGHT
○ HAZY	○ MEDIUM
○ OVERCAST	○ HEAVY
○ CHANGING	○ OTHER

12 9 3 6

12 9 3 6

NOTES

| OVERALL RESULTS | ○ POOR ○ FAIR ○ GOOD ○ EXCELLENT | ☆ ☆ ☆ ☆ ☆ |

◎ TARGET SIZE _____

TARGET _____

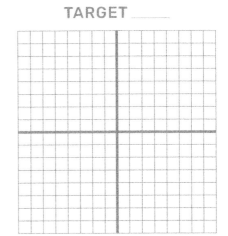

TARGET _____

TARGET _____

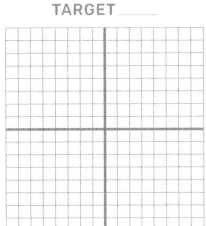

TARGET _____

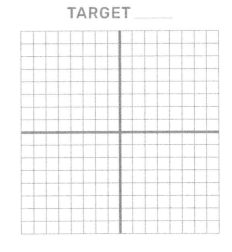

TARGET _____

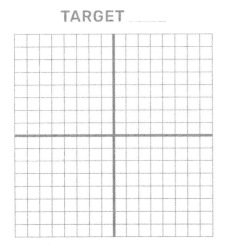

TARGET _____

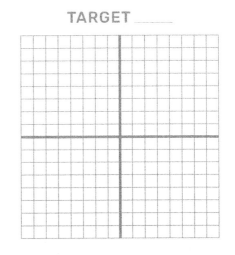

SHOOTING Log Book

SHOOTING

DATE	Ⓜ Ⓣ Ⓦ Ⓣ Ⓕ Ⓢ Ⓢ TIME
LOCATION	
FIREARM	
RIFLE/SCOPE	
AMMUNITION	
SEATING DEPTH	
DISTANCE	
POWDER	GRAINS
PRIMER	
BRASS	

CONDITIONS

LIGHT	WIND
○ BRIGHT	○ LIGHT
○ HAZY	○ MEDIUM
○ OVERCAST	○ HEAVY
○ CHANGING	○ OTHER

LIGHT clock: 12, 3, 6, 9

WIND clock: 12, 3, 6, 9

NOTES

OVERALL RESULTS	○ POOR ○ FAIR ○ GOOD ○ EXCELLENT	☆ ☆ ☆ ☆ ☆

TARGET _____

TARGET _____

TARGET _____

TARGET _____

TARGET _____

TARGET _____

SHOOTING *Log Book*

SHOOTING

DATE	Ⓜ Ⓣ Ⓦ Ⓣ Ⓕ Ⓢ Ⓢ TIME
LOCATION	
FIREARM	
RIFLE/SCOPE	
AMMUNITION	
SEATING DEPTH	
DISTANCE	
POWDER	GRAINS
PRIMER	
BRASS	

CONDITIONS

LIGHT	WIND
○ BRIGHT	○ LIGHT
○ HAZY	○ MEDIUM
○ OVERCAST	○ HEAVY
○ CHANGING	○ OTHER

NOTES

OVERALL RESULTS	○ POOR ○ FAIR ○ GOOD ○ EXCELLENT ☆ ☆ ☆ ☆ ☆

◉ TARGET SIZE _____

TARGET _____

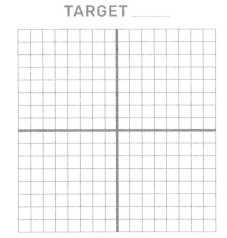

TARGET _____

TARGET _____

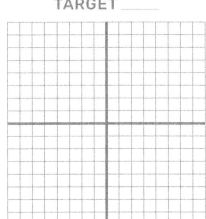

TARGET _____

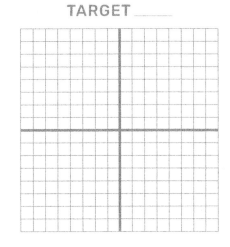

TARGET _____

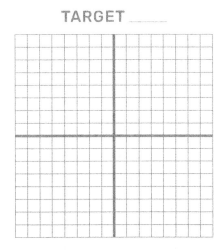

TARGET _____

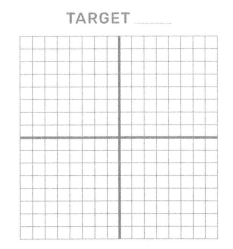

SHOOTING *Log Book*

SHOOTING

DATE	Ⓜ Ⓣ Ⓦ Ⓣ Ⓕ Ⓢ Ⓢ TIME
LOCATION	
FIREARM	
RIFLE/SCOPE	
AMMUNITION	
SEATING DEPTH	
DISTANCE	
POWDER	GRAINS
PRIMER	
BRASS	

CONDITIONS

LIGHT	WIND
○ BRIGHT	○ LIGHT
○ HAZY	○ MEDIUM
○ OVERCAST	○ HEAVY
○ CHANGING	○ OTHER

LIGHT clock: 12, 3, 6, 9

WIND clock: 12, 3, 6, 9

NOTES

OVERALL RESULTS	○ POOR ○ FAIR ○ GOOD ○ EXCELLENT ☆ ☆ ☆ ☆ ☆

◉ TARGET SIZE _____

TARGET _____

TARGET _____

TARGET _____

TARGET _____

TARGET _____

TARGET _____

SHOOTING *Log Book*

SHOOTING

DATE	Ⓜ Ⓣ Ⓦ Ⓣ Ⓕ Ⓢ Ⓢ	**TIME**
LOCATION		
FIREARM		
RIFLE/SCOPE		
AMMUNITION		
SEATING DEPTH		
DISTANCE		
POWDER	GRAINS	
PRIMER		
BRASS		

CONDITIONS

LIGHT	WIND
○ BRIGHT	○ LIGHT
○ HAZY	○ MEDIUM
○ OVERCAST	○ HEAVY
○ CHANGING	○ OTHER

(Light clock face: 12, 3, 6, 9)
(Wind clock face: 12, 3, 6, 9)

NOTES

OVERALL RESULTS ○ POOR ○ FAIR ○ GOOD ○ EXCELLENT ☆ ☆ ☆ ☆ ☆

◎ TARGET SIZE _____

TARGET _____

TARGET _____

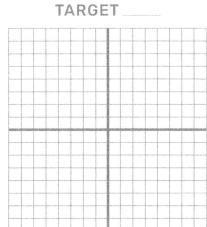

TARGET _____

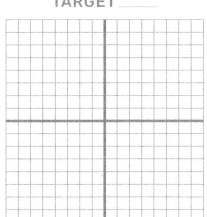

TARGET _____

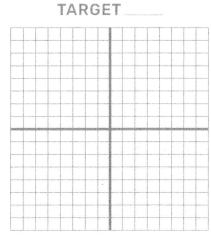

TARGET _____

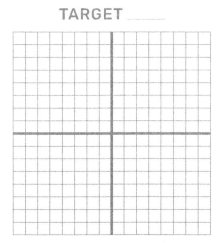

TARGET _____

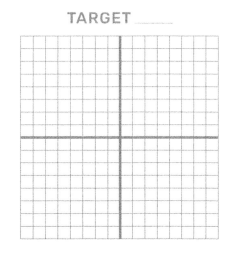

SHOOTING *Log Book*

SHOOTING

DATE	ⓂⓉⓌⓉⒻⓈⓈ	TIME
LOCATION		
FIREARM		
RIFLE/SCOPE		
AMMUNITION		
SEATING DEPTH		
DISTANCE		
POWDER	GRAINS	
PRIMER		
BRASS		

CONDITIONS

LIGHT	WIND
○ BRIGHT	○ LIGHT
○ HAZY	○ MEDIUM
○ OVERCAST	○ HEAVY
○ CHANGING	○ OTHER

(clock faces: 12, 3, 6, 9)

NOTES

OVERALL RESULTS ○ POOR ○ FAIR ○ GOOD ○ EXCELLENT ☆ ☆ ☆ ☆ ☆

TARGET _____

TARGET _____

TARGET _____

TARGET _____

TARGET _____

TARGET _____

SHOOTING Log Book

SHOOTING

DATE	Ⓜ Ⓣ Ⓦ Ⓣ Ⓕ Ⓢ Ⓢ	TIME	
LOCATION			
FIREARM			
RIFLE/SCOPE			
AMMUNITION			
SEATING DEPTH			
DISTANCE			
POWDER		GRAINS	
PRIMER			
BRASS			

CONDITIONS

LIGHT	WIND
○ BRIGHT	○ LIGHT
○ HAZY	○ MEDIUM
○ OVERCAST	○ HEAVY
○ CHANGING	○ OTHER

LIGHT clock: 12 / 3 / 6 / 9

WIND clock: 12 / 3 / 6 / 9

NOTES

OVERALL RESULTS	○ POOR ○ FAIR ○ GOOD ○ EXCELLENT	☆ ☆ ☆ ☆ ☆

TARGET _____

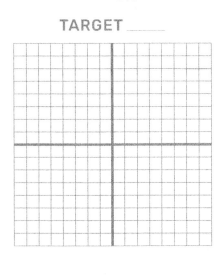

TARGET _____

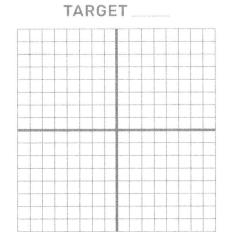

TARGET _____

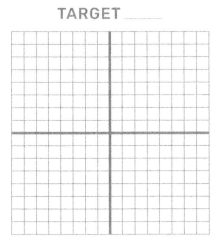

TARGET _____

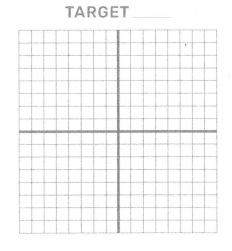

TARGET _____

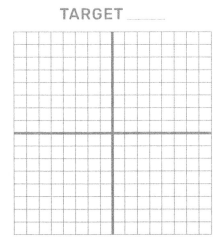

TARGET _____

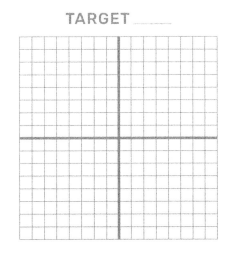

SHOOTING *Log Book*

SHOOTING

DATE	Ⓜ Ⓣ Ⓦ Ⓣ Ⓕ Ⓢ Ⓢ TIME
LOCATION	
FIREARM	
RIFLE/SCOPE	
AMMUNITION	
SEATING DEPTH	
DISTANCE	
POWDER	GRAINS
PRIMER	
BRASS	

CONDITIONS

LIGHT	WIND
○ BRIGHT	○ LIGHT
○ HAZY	○ MEDIUM
○ OVERCAST	○ HEAVY
○ CHANGING	○ OTHER

(Light clock: 12, 3, 6, 9) (Wind clock: 12, 3, 6, 9)

NOTES

OVERALL RESULTS | ○ POOR ○ FAIR ○ GOOD ○ EXCELLENT ☆ ☆ ☆ ☆ ☆

TARGET _____

TARGET _____

TARGET _____

TARGET _____

TARGET _____

TARGET _____

SHOOTING Log Book

SHOOTING

DATE	Ⓜ Ⓣ Ⓦ Ⓣ Ⓕ Ⓢ Ⓢ TIME
LOCATION	
FIREARM	
RIFLE/SCOPE	
AMMUNITION	
SEATING DEPTH	
DISTANCE	
POWDER	GRAINS
PRIMER	
BRASS	

CONDITIONS

LIGHT	WIND
○ BRIGHT	○ LIGHT
○ HAZY	○ MEDIUM
○ OVERCAST	○ HEAVY
○ CHANGING	○ OTHER

LIGHT clock: 12, 3, 6, 9

WIND clock: 12, 3, 6, 9

NOTES

OVERALL RESULTS	○ POOR ○ FAIR ○ GOOD ○ EXCELLENT	☆ ☆ ☆ ☆ ☆

TARGET _____

TARGET _____

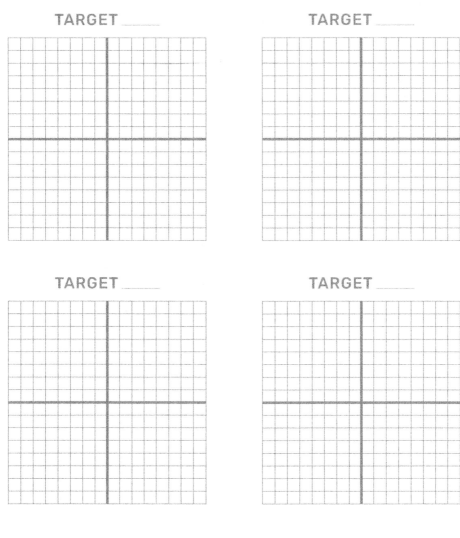

TARGET _____

TARGET _____

TARGET _____

TARGET _____

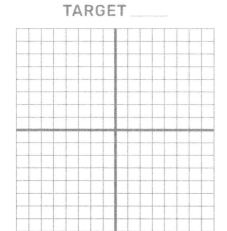
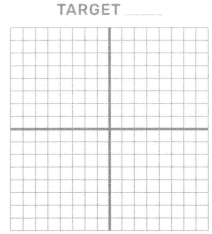

SHOOTING *Log Book*

SHOOTING

DATE	Ⓜ Ⓣ Ⓦ Ⓣ Ⓕ Ⓢ Ⓢ TIME
LOCATION	
FIREARM	
RIFLE/SCOPE	
AMMUNITION	
SEATING DEPTH	
DISTANCE	
POWDER	GRAINS
PRIMER	
BRASS	

CONDITIONS

LIGHT	WIND
○ BRIGHT ○ HAZY ○ OVERCAST ○ CHANGING	○ LIGHT ○ MEDIUM ○ HEAVY ○ OTHER

(Light clock: 12, 3, 6, 9)   (Wind clock: 12, 3, 6, 9)

NOTES

OVERALL RESULTS	○ POOR ○ FAIR ○ GOOD ○ EXCELLENT ☆ ☆ ☆ ☆ ☆

◎ TARGET SIZE _____

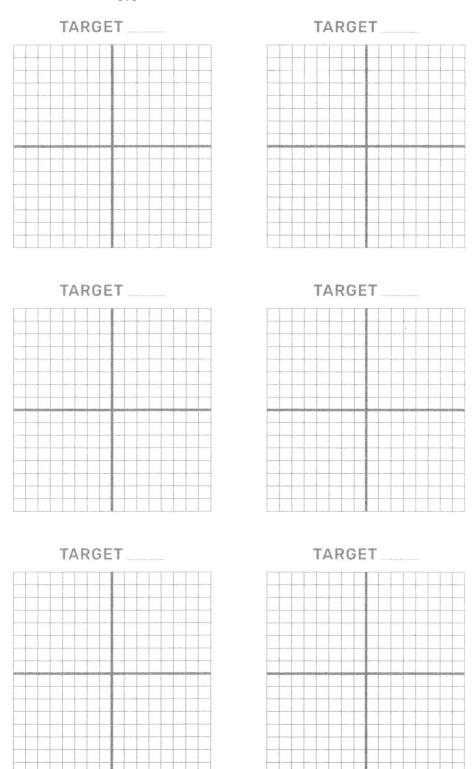

TARGET _____

TARGET _____

TARGET _____

TARGET _____

TARGET _____

TARGET _____

SHOOTING *Log Book*

SHOOTING

DATE	Ⓜ Ⓣ Ⓦ Ⓣ Ⓕ Ⓢ Ⓢ TIME
LOCATION	
FIREARM	
RIFLE/SCOPE	
AMMUNITION	
SEATING DEPTH	
DISTANCE	
POWDER	GRAINS
PRIMER	
BRASS	

CONDITIONS

LIGHT	WIND
○ BRIGHT	○ LIGHT
○ HAZY	○ MEDIUM
○ OVERCAST	○ HEAVY
○ CHANGING	○ OTHER

12
9   3
6

12
9   3
6

NOTES

OVERALL RESULTS	○ POOR ○ FAIR ○ GOOD ○ EXCELLENT	☆ ☆ ☆ ☆ ☆

◎ TARGET SIZE _____

TARGET _____

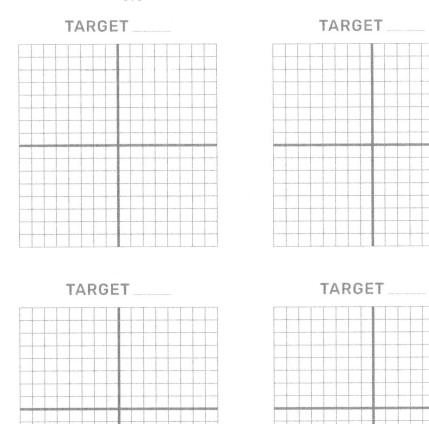

TARGET _____

TARGET _____

TARGET _____

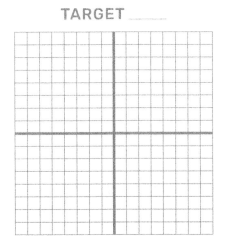

TARGET _____

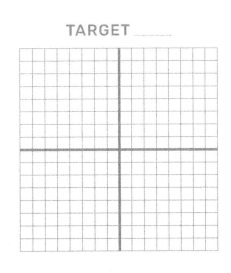

SHOOTING *Log Book*

SHOOTING

DATE	Ⓜ Ⓣ Ⓦ Ⓣ Ⓕ Ⓢ Ⓢ TIME
LOCATION	
FIREARM	
RIFLE/SCOPE	
AMMUNITION	
SEATING DEPTH	
DISTANCE	
POWDER	GRAINS
PRIMER	
BRASS	

CONDITIONS

LIGHT	WIND
○ BRIGHT	○ LIGHT
○ HAZY	○ MEDIUM
○ OVERCAST	○ HEAVY
○ CHANGING	○ OTHER

12 / 9 / 3 / 6

12 / 9 / 3 / 6

NOTES

OVERALL RESULTS | ○ POOR ○ FAIR ○ GOOD ○ EXCELLENT ☆ ☆ ☆ ☆ ☆

TARGET _____

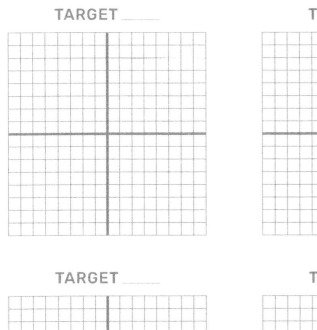

TARGET _____

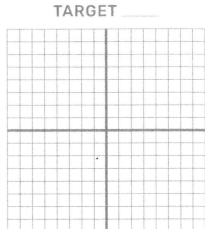

TARGET _____

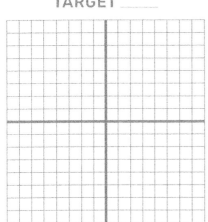

TARGET _____

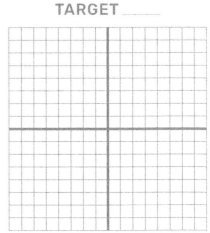

TARGET _____

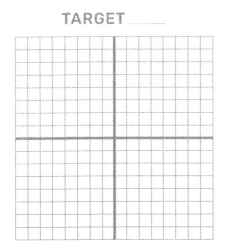

TARGET _____

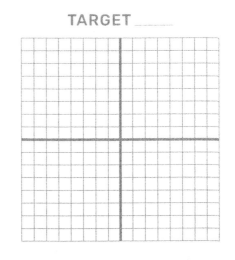

SHOOTING *Log Book*

SHOOTING

DATE	(M)(T)(W)(T)(F)(S)(S) **TIME**
LOCATION	
FIREARM	
RIFLE/SCOPE	
AMMUNITION	
SEATING DEPTH	
DISTANCE	
POWDER	GRAINS
PRIMER	
BRASS	

CONDITIONS

LIGHT	WIND
○ BRIGHT	○ LIGHT
○ HAZY	○ MEDIUM
○ OVERCAST	○ HEAVY
○ CHANGING	○ OTHER

12 9 3 6

12 9 3 6

NOTES

OVERALL RESULTS | ○ POOR ○ FAIR ○ GOOD ○ EXCELLENT ☆ ☆ ☆ ☆ ☆

TARGET _____

TARGET _____

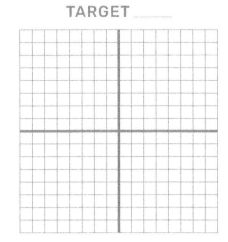

TARGET _____

TARGET _____

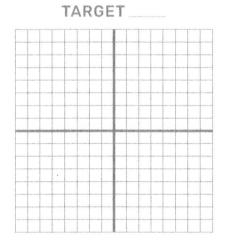

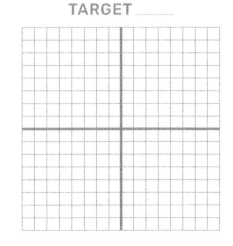

TARGET _____

TARGET _____

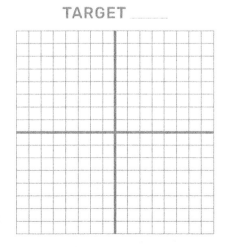

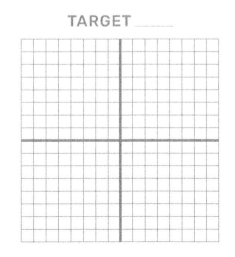

SHOOTING *Log Book*

SHOOTING

DATE	Ⓜ Ⓣ Ⓦ Ⓣ Ⓕ Ⓢ Ⓢ TIME
LOCATION	
FIREARM	
RIFLE/SCOPE	
AMMUNITION	
SEATING DEPTH	
DISTANCE	
POWDER	GRAINS
PRIMER	
BRASS	

CONDITIONS

LIGHT	WIND
○ BRIGHT	○ LIGHT
○ HAZY	○ MEDIUM
○ OVERCAST	○ HEAVY
○ CHANGING	○ OTHER

12
9   3
6

12
9   3
6

NOTES

OVERALL RESULTS ○ POOR ○ FAIR ○ GOOD ○ EXCELLENT ☆ ☆ ☆ ☆ ☆

TARGET _____

TARGET _____

TARGET _____

TARGET _____

TARGET _____

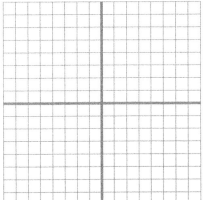

TARGET _____

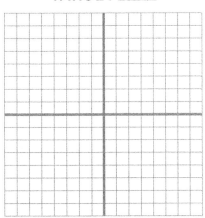

SHOOTING $\mathcal{Log}$ $\mathcal{Book}$

SHOOTING

DATE	Ⓜ Ⓣ Ⓦ Ⓣ Ⓕ Ⓢ Ⓢ **TIME**
LOCATION	
FIREARM	
RIFLE/SCOPE	
AMMUNITION	
SEATING DEPTH	
DISTANCE	
POWDER	GRAINS
PRIMER	
BRASS	

CONDITIONS

LIGHT	WIND
○ BRIGHT	○ LIGHT
○ HAZY	○ MEDIUM
○ OVERCAST	○ HEAVY
○ CHANGING	○ OTHER

(clock face: 12, 3, 6, 9)   (clock face: 12, 3, 6, 9)

NOTES

OVERALL RESULTS	○ POOR ○ FAIR ○ GOOD ○ EXCELLENT	☆ ☆ ☆ ☆ ☆

◎ TARGET SIZE _____

TARGET _____

TARGET _____

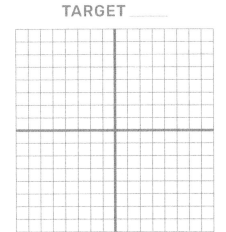

TARGET _____

TARGET _____

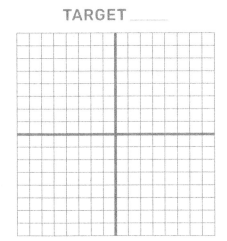

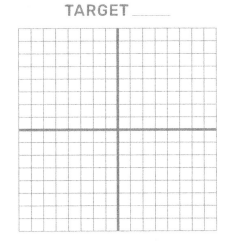

TARGET _____

TARGET _____

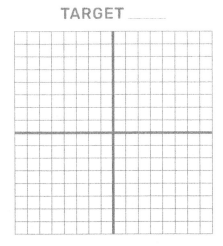

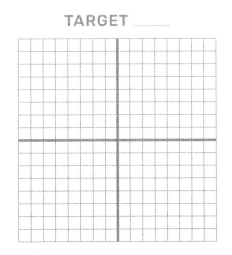

SHOOTING *Log Book*

SHOOTING

DATE		M T W T F S S	TIME
LOCATION			
FIREARM			
RIFLE/SCOPE			
AMMUNITION			
SEATING DEPTH			
DISTANCE			
POWDER		GRAINS	
PRIMER			
BRASS			

CONDITIONS

LIGHT	WIND
○ BRIGHT	○ LIGHT
○ HAZY	○ MEDIUM
○ OVERCAST	○ HEAVY
○ CHANGING	○ OTHER

LIGHT clock: 12, 9, 3, 6

WIND clock: 12, 9, 3, 6

NOTES

OVERALL RESULTS	○ POOR ○ FAIR ○ GOOD ○ EXCELLENT ☆ ☆ ☆ ☆ ☆

TARGET _____

TARGET _____

TARGET _____

TARGET _____

TARGET _____

TARGET _____

SHOOTING Log Book

SHOOTING

DATE	Ⓜ Ⓣ Ⓦ Ⓣ Ⓕ Ⓢ Ⓢ	TIME	
LOCATION			
FIREARM			
RIFLE/SCOPE			
AMMUNITION			
SEATING DEPTH			
DISTANCE			
POWDER		GRAINS	
PRIMER			
BRASS			

CONDITIONS

LIGHT	WIND
○ BRIGHT	○ LIGHT
○ HAZY	○ MEDIUM
○ OVERCAST	○ HEAVY
○ CHANGING	○ OTHER

12 · 9 · 3 · 6   12 · 9 · 3 · 6

NOTES

OVERALL RESULTS	○ POOR ○ FAIR ○ GOOD ○ EXCELLENT ☆ ☆ ☆ ☆ ☆

TARGET ___

TARGET ___

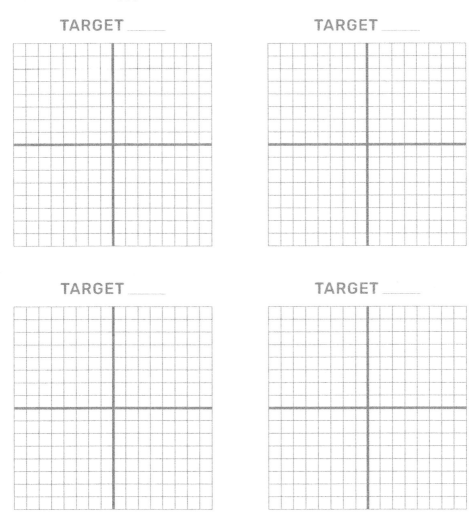

TARGET ___

TARGET ___

TARGET ___

TARGET ___

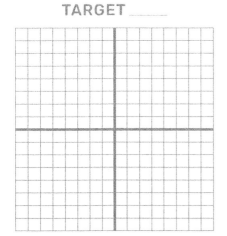
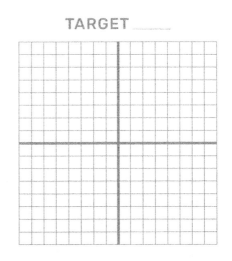

SHOOTING *Log Book*

SHOOTING

DATE	Ⓜ Ⓣ Ⓦ Ⓣ Ⓕ Ⓢ Ⓢ **TIME**
LOCATION	
FIREARM	
RIFLE/SCOPE	
AMMUNITION	
SEATING DEPTH	
DISTANCE	
POWDER	GRAINS
PRIMER	
BRASS	

CONDITIONS

LIGHT	WIND
○ BRIGHT	○ LIGHT
○ HAZY	○ MEDIUM
○ OVERCAST	○ HEAVY
○ CHANGING	○ OTHER

(LIGHT clock: 12, 3, 6, 9) (WIND clock: 12, 3, 6, 9)

NOTES

OVERALL RESULTS	○ POOR ○ FAIR ○ GOOD ○ EXCELLENT ☆ ☆ ☆ ☆ ☆

TARGET _____

TARGET _____

TARGET _____

TARGET _____

TARGET _____

TARGET _____

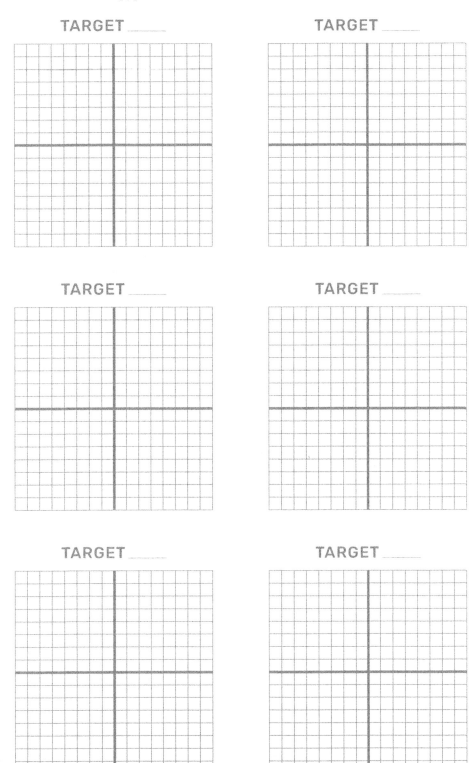

SHOOTING $\mathcal{Log}$ $\mathcal{Book}$

SHOOTING

DATE	Ⓜ Ⓣ Ⓦ Ⓣ Ⓕ Ⓢ Ⓢ **TIME**
LOCATION	
FIREARM	
RIFLE/SCOPE	
AMMUNITION	
SEATING DEPTH	
DISTANCE	
POWDER	GRAINS
PRIMER	
BRASS	

CONDITIONS

LIGHT	WIND
○ BRIGHT	○ LIGHT
○ HAZY	○ MEDIUM
○ OVERCAST	○ HEAVY
○ CHANGING	○ OTHER

NOTES

OVERALL RESULTS	○ POOR ○ FAIR ○ GOOD ○ EXCELLENT	☆ ☆ ☆ ☆ ☆

TARGET _____

TARGET _____

TARGET _____

TARGET _____

TARGET _____

TARGET _____

SHOOTING *Log Book*

SHOOTING

DATE	Ⓜ Ⓣ Ⓦ Ⓣ Ⓕ Ⓢ Ⓢ TIME
LOCATION	
FIREARM	
RIFLE/SCOPE	
AMMUNITION	
SEATING DEPTH	
DISTANCE	
POWDER	GRAINS
PRIMER	
BRASS	

CONDITIONS

LIGHT	WIND
○ BRIGHT	○ LIGHT
○ HAZY	○ MEDIUM
○ OVERCAST	○ HEAVY
○ CHANGING	○ OTHER

12
9   3
6

12
9   3
6

NOTES

OVERALL RESULTS	○ POOR ○ FAIR ○ GOOD ○ EXCELLENT	☆ ☆ ☆ ☆ ☆

⊚ TARGET SIZE _____

TARGET _____

TARGET _____

TARGET _____

TARGET _____

TARGET _____

TARGET _____

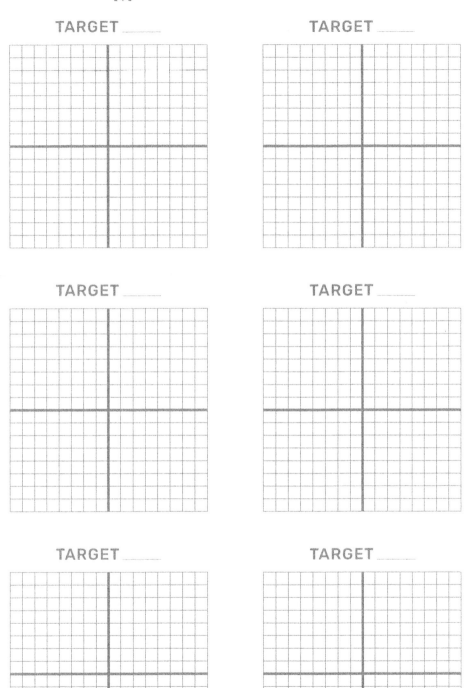

SHOOTING $\mathcal{Log}$ $\mathcal{Book}$

SHOOTING

DATE	Ⓜ Ⓣ Ⓦ Ⓣ Ⓕ Ⓢ Ⓢ **TIME**
LOCATION	
FIREARM	
RIFLE/SCOPE	
AMMUNITION	
SEATING DEPTH	
DISTANCE	
POWDER	GRAINS
PRIMER	
BRASS	

CONDITIONS

LIGHT	WIND
○ BRIGHT	○ LIGHT
○ HAZY	○ MEDIUM
○ OVERCAST	○ HEAVY
○ CHANGING	○ OTHER

LIGHT clock: 12 / 3 / 6 / 9

WIND clock: 12 / 3 / 6 / 9

NOTES

OVERALL RESULTS	○ POOR ○ FAIR ○ GOOD ○ EXCELLENT	☆ ☆ ☆ ☆ ☆

⊚ TARGET SIZE _____

TARGET _____

TARGET _____

TARGET _____

TARGET _____

TARGET _____

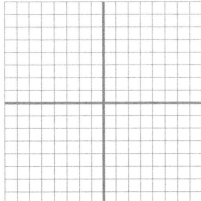

TARGET _____

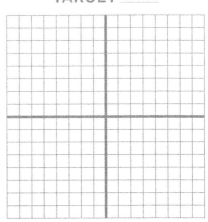

SHOOTING *Log Book*

SHOOTING

DATE	Ⓜ Ⓣ Ⓦ Ⓣ Ⓕ Ⓢ Ⓢ TIME
LOCATION	
FIREARM	
RIFLE/SCOPE	
AMMUNITION	
SEATING DEPTH	
DISTANCE	
POWDER	GRAINS
PRIMER	
BRASS	

CONDITIONS

LIGHT	WIND
○ BRIGHT	○ LIGHT
○ HAZY	○ MEDIUM
○ OVERCAST	○ HEAVY
○ CHANGING	○ OTHER

12
9   3
6

12
9   3
6

NOTES

OVERALL RESULTS	○ POOR ○ FAIR ○ GOOD ○ EXCELLENT ☆ ☆ ☆ ☆ ☆

TARGET _____

TARGET _____

TARGET _____

TARGET _____

TARGET _____

TARGET _____

SHOOTING $\mathcal{Log}$ Book

SHOOTING

DATE	Ⓜ Ⓣ Ⓦ Ⓣ Ⓕ Ⓢ Ⓢ	TIME	
LOCATION			
FIREARM			
RIFLE/SCOPE			
AMMUNITION			
SEATING DEPTH			
DISTANCE			
POWDER	GRAINS		
PRIMER			
BRASS			

CONDITIONS

LIGHT	WIND
○ BRIGHT	○ LIGHT
○ HAZY	○ MEDIUM
○ OVERCAST	○ HEAVY
○ CHANGING	○ OTHER

(Light clock: 12, 3, 6, 9) (Wind clock: 12, 3, 6, 9)

NOTES

OVERALL RESULTS	○ POOR ○ FAIR ○ GOOD ○ EXCELLENT	☆ ☆ ☆ ☆ ☆

◎ TARGET SIZE _____

TARGET _____

TARGET _____

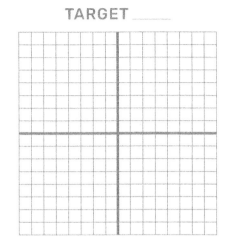

TARGET _____

TARGET _____

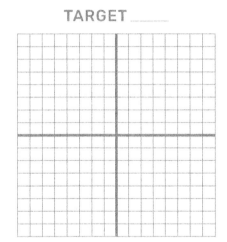

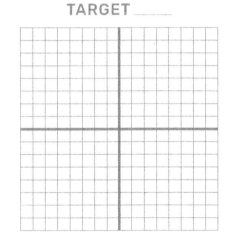

TARGET _____

TARGET _____

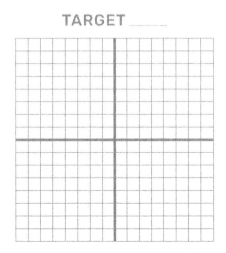

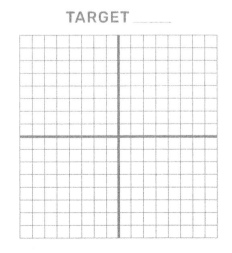

SHOOTING *Log Book*

SHOOTING

DATE	Ⓜ Ⓣ Ⓦ Ⓣ Ⓕ Ⓢ Ⓢ	TIME
LOCATION		
FIREARM		
RIFLE/SCOPE		
AMMUNITION		
SEATING DEPTH		
DISTANCE		
POWDER	GRAINS	
PRIMER		
BRASS		

CONDITIONS

LIGHT	WIND
○ BRIGHT	○ LIGHT
○ HAZY	○ MEDIUM
○ OVERCAST	○ HEAVY
○ CHANGING	○ OTHER

NOTES

OVERALL RESULTS	○ POOR ○ FAIR ○ GOOD ○ EXCELLENT	☆ ☆ ☆ ☆ ☆

TARGET _____

TARGET _____

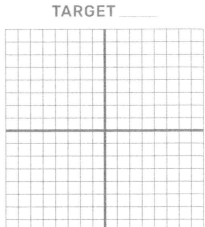

TARGET _____

TARGET _____

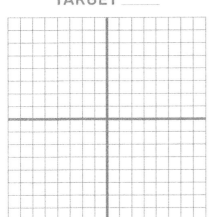

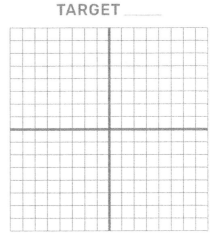

TARGET _____

TARGET _____

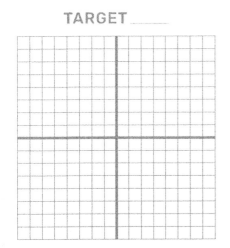

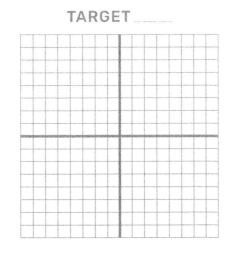

SHOOTING Log Book

SHOOTING

DATE	Ⓜ Ⓣ Ⓦ Ⓣ Ⓕ Ⓢ Ⓢ	TIME
LOCATION		
FIREARM		
RIFLE/SCOPE		
AMMUNITION		
SEATING DEPTH		
DISTANCE		
POWDER	GRAINS	
PRIMER		
BRASS		

CONDITIONS

LIGHT	WIND
○ BRIGHT	○ LIGHT
○ HAZY	○ MEDIUM
○ OVERCAST	○ HEAVY
○ CHANGING	○ OTHER

LIGHT clock: 12, 3, 6, 9

WIND clock: 12, 3, 6, 9

NOTES

OVERALL RESULTS	○ POOR ○ FAIR ○ GOOD ○ EXCELLENT	☆ ☆ ☆ ☆ ☆

TARGET _____

TARGET _____

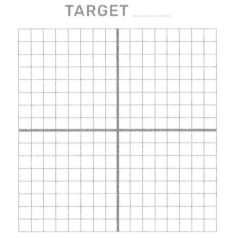

TARGET _____

TARGET _____

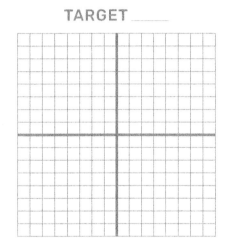
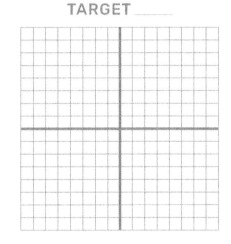

TARGET _____

TARGET _____

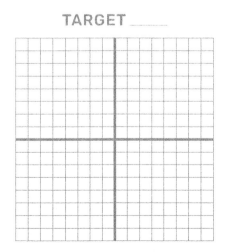
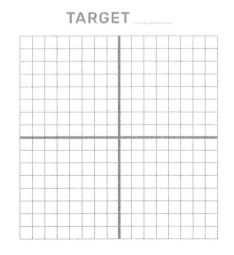

SHOOTING $\mathcal{Log}$ $\mathcal{Book}$

SHOOTING

DATE	Ⓜ Ⓣ Ⓦ Ⓣ Ⓕ Ⓢ Ⓢ	TIME
LOCATION		
FIREARM		
RIFLE/SCOPE		
AMMUNITION		
SEATING DEPTH		
DISTANCE		
POWDER	GRAINS	
PRIMER		
BRASS		

CONDITIONS

LIGHT	WIND
○ BRIGHT	○ LIGHT
○ HAZY	○ MEDIUM
○ OVERCAST	○ HEAVY
○ CHANGING	○ OTHER

LIGHT clock: 12, 3, 6, 9
WIND clock: 12, 3, 6, 9

NOTES

OVERALL RESULTS | ○ POOR ○ FAIR ○ GOOD ○ EXCELLENT | ☆ ☆ ☆ ☆ ☆

TARGET _____

TARGET _____

TARGET _____

TARGET _____

TARGET _____

TARGET _____

SHOOTING *Log Book*

SHOOTING

DATE	Ⓜ Ⓣ Ⓦ Ⓣ Ⓕ Ⓢ Ⓢ TIME
LOCATION	
FIREARM	
RIFLE/SCOPE	
AMMUNITION	
SEATING DEPTH	
DISTANCE	
POWDER	GRAINS
PRIMER	
BRASS	

CONDITIONS

LIGHT	WIND
○ BRIGHT	○ LIGHT
○ HAZY	○ MEDIUM
○ OVERCAST	○ HEAVY
○ CHANGING	○ OTHER

(clock: 12, 3, 6, 9)

NOTES

OVERALL RESULTS ○ POOR ○ FAIR ○ GOOD ○ EXCELLENT ☆ ☆ ☆ ☆ ☆

◎ TARGET SIZE _____

TARGET _____

TARGET _____

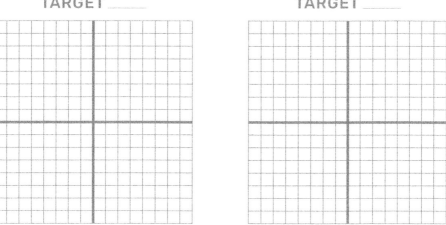

TARGET _____

TARGET _____

TARGET _____

TARGET _____

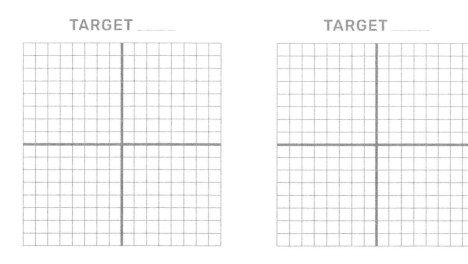

SHOOTING $\mathcal{Log}$ $\mathcal{Book}$

SHOOTING

DATE	Ⓜ Ⓣ Ⓦ Ⓣ Ⓕ Ⓢ Ⓢ TIME
LOCATION	
FIREARM	
RIFLE/SCOPE	
AMMUNITION	
SEATING DEPTH	
DISTANCE	
POWDER	GRAINS
PRIMER	
BRASS	

CONDITIONS

LIGHT	WIND
○ BRIGHT	○ LIGHT
○ HAZY	○ MEDIUM
○ OVERCAST	○ HEAVY
○ CHANGING	○ OTHER

NOTES

OVERALL RESULTS	○ POOR ○ FAIR ○ GOOD ○ EXCELLENT	☆ ☆ ☆ ☆ ☆

TARGET _____

TARGET _____

TARGET _____

TARGET _____

TARGET _____

TARGET _____

SHOOTING *Log Book*

SHOOTING

DATE		M T W T F S S	TIME	
LOCATION				
FIREARM				
RIFLE/SCOPE				
AMMUNITION				
SEATING DEPTH				
DISTANCE				
POWDER		GRAINS		
PRIMER				
BRASS				

CONDITIONS

LIGHT		WIND	
○ BRIGHT	12	○ LIGHT	12
○ HAZY	9 3	○ MEDIUM	9 3
○ OVERCAST		○ HEAVY	
○ CHANGING	6	○ OTHER	6

NOTES

OVERALL RESULTS	○ POOR ○ FAIR ○ GOOD ○ EXCELLENT	☆ ☆ ☆ ☆ ☆

◎ TARGET SIZE _____

TARGET _____

TARGET _____

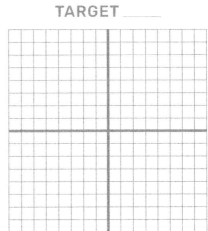

TARGET _____

TARGET _____

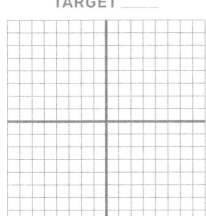

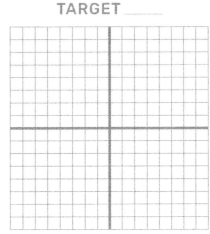

TARGET _____

TARGET _____

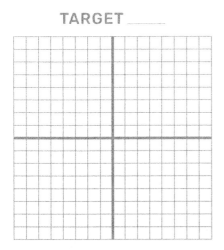

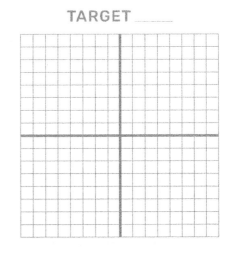

SHOOTING *Log Book*

SHOOTING

DATE	Ⓜ Ⓣ Ⓦ Ⓣ Ⓕ Ⓢ Ⓢ TIME
LOCATION	
FIREARM	
RIFLE/SCOPE	
AMMUNITION	
SEATING DEPTH	
DISTANCE	
POWDER	GRAINS
PRIMER	
BRASS	

CONDITIONS

LIGHT	WIND
○ BRIGHT	○ LIGHT
○ HAZY	○ MEDIUM
○ OVERCAST	○ HEAVY
○ CHANGING	○ OTHER

12
9   3
6

12
9   3
6

NOTES

OVERALL RESULTS	○ POOR ○ FAIR ○ GOOD ○ EXCELLENT	☆ ☆ ☆ ☆ ☆

TARGET _____

TARGET _____

TARGET _____

TARGET _____

TARGET _____

TARGET _____

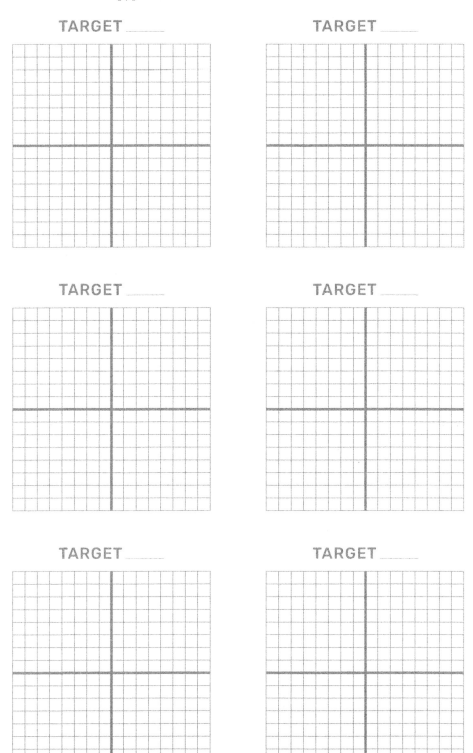

SHOOTING Log Book

SHOOTING

DATE	Ⓜ Ⓣ Ⓦ Ⓣ Ⓕ Ⓢ Ⓢ TIME
LOCATION	
FIREARM	
RIFLE/SCOPE	
AMMUNITION	
SEATING DEPTH	
DISTANCE	
POWDER	GRAINS
PRIMER	
BRASS	

CONDITIONS

LIGHT	WIND
○ BRIGHT	○ LIGHT
○ HAZY	○ MEDIUM
○ OVERCAST	○ HEAVY
○ CHANGING	○ OTHER

12 9 3 6

12 9 3 6

NOTES

OVERALL RESULTS	○ POOR ○ FAIR ○ GOOD ○ EXCELLENT ☆ ☆ ☆ ☆ ☆

TARGET _____

TARGET _____

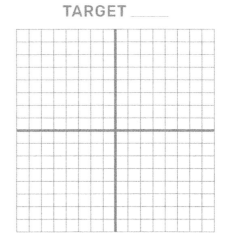

TARGET _____

TARGET _____

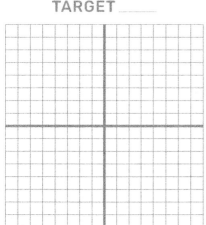

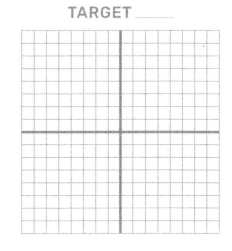

TARGET _____

TARGET _____

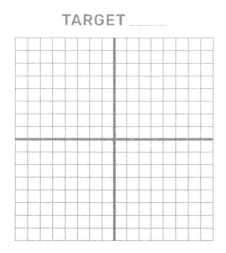

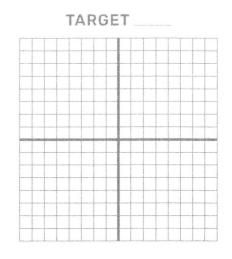

SHOOTING Log $Book$

SHOOTING

DATE	Ⓜ Ⓣ Ⓦ Ⓣ Ⓕ Ⓢ Ⓢ TIME
LOCATION	
FIREARM	
RIFLE/SCOPE	
AMMUNITION	
SEATING DEPTH	
DISTANCE	
POWDER	GRAINS
PRIMER	
BRASS	

CONDITIONS

LIGHT	WIND
○ BRIGHT	○ LIGHT
○ HAZY	○ MEDIUM
○ OVERCAST	○ HEAVY
○ CHANGING	○ OTHER

12 9 3 6

12 9 3 6

NOTES

OVERALL RESULTS	○ POOR ○ FAIR ○ GOOD ○ EXCELLENT ☆ ☆ ☆ ☆ ☆

◉ TARGET SIZE _____

TARGET _____

TARGET _____

TARGET _____

TARGET _____

TARGET _____

TARGET _____

SHOOTING *Log Book*

SHOOTING

DATE	Ⓜ Ⓣ Ⓦ Ⓣ Ⓕ Ⓢ Ⓢ **TIME**
LOCATION	
FIREARM	
RIFLE/SCOPE	
AMMUNITION	
SEATING DEPTH	
DISTANCE	
POWDER	GRAINS
PRIMER	
BRASS	

CONDITIONS

LIGHT	WIND
○ BRIGHT	○ LIGHT
○ HAZY	○ MEDIUM
○ OVERCAST	○ HEAVY
○ CHANGING	○ OTHER

12 · 9 · 3 · 6 (LIGHT)

12 · 9 · 3 · 6 (WIND)

NOTES

OVERALL RESULTS	○ POOR ○ FAIR ○ GOOD ○ EXCELLENT	☆ ☆ ☆ ☆ ☆

TARGET _____

TARGET _____

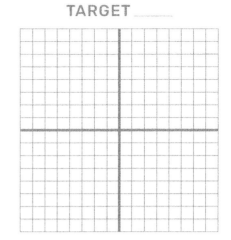

TARGET _____

TARGET _____

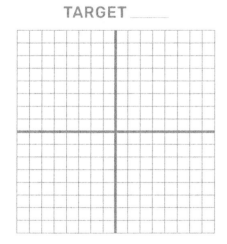

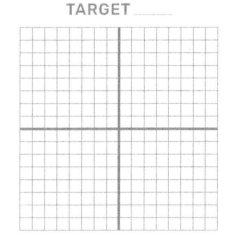

TARGET _____

TARGET _____

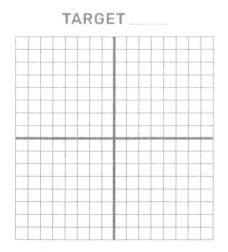

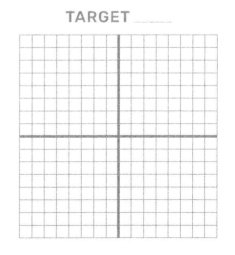

Made in United States
North Haven, CT
01 February 2024

48178679R10063